*We have this hope—*

*like a sure and firm anchor of the soul.*

HEBREWS 6:19 (HCSB)

*"Anchors of Hope* is the book I've been waiting for Sandi Banks to write. She lives the truth that 'beauty comes wrapped in the thorns of our lives,' and her stories of God's strengthening presence will encourage hurting hearts."

Sandra P. Aldrich, speaker and author

"With gentle narrative and vivid images, Sandi passes on the comfort with which she has indeed been comforted. The hope that God has shone in her heart reflects off each page."

Lael Arrington, author, *Worldproofing Your Kids*

"Sandi's book is a must-read for all us who have discovered that life isn't fair. It's my new favorite gift for friends who are experiencing difficult circumstances, unanswered prayer, personal betrayal, or unexplained loss. *Anchors of Hope* brings waves of fresh faith into storm-filled lives."

Carol Kent, president, Speak Up Speaker Services
author, *Becoming a Woman of Influence*

"You will feel as though you and Sandi were having coffee together and she was personally sharing a message of hope with you through her experiences, stories, and insights into Scripture. I loved this book— and so will you!"

Carole Mayhall, author, *Words That Hurt, Words That Heal*

"Sandi Banks has hit the mark. She writes with wisdom, sensitivity and humor about life's deepest struggles. She guides us in discovering our hope in God and His word. Every paragraph will lead to personal encouragement and authentic spiritual growth."

Mary White, author, *Harsh Grief, Gentle Hope*

# ANCHORS
*of*
# HOPE

*finding peace*
*amidst the storms of life*

## SANDI BANKS

Broadman & Holman Publishers
Nashville, Tennessee

Broadman & Holman Publishers
Nashville, Tennessee
Printed in Belgium
ISBN 0-8054-9515-0

Names have been changed where necessary to honor confidentialities.

References to deity are capitalized throughout this book, including quotes from other sources as well as Scripture versions which use lower case.

# FOREWORD

For over twenty years I have been privileged to be a small part of Sandi Banks' life. One of my first memories of Sandi is of her leading worship at our women's ministry meeting. Her sweet spirit and continual smile made our worship extra special. I discovered that she and her family were in Tucson because her husband, who was in the military, had been transferred to Davis-Monthan Air Force Base. Since my husband, Jack, and I were ministering at the base, it was natural and God-ordained that we decided to meet regularly for fellowship and encouragement.

This was the beginning of my special friendship with Sandi. The Good Earth restaurant became our shelter, tea our beverage of choice, and the Bible our book. Talk, teaching, and tears made up our agenda. Sandi's desire to grow and please God was evident from our first meeting, and it was with joy that I watched her quickly embrace the truth of Scripture for her life. These truths took deep root in the good soil of her heart and have since blossomed and borne fruit as they have been watered and nourished by both sweet and bitter water.

Sandi has learned to drink from the fountain of God's sovereignty and to humbly accept troubled waters as part of her journey.

She has become a skillful sailor and has discovered and clung to the secure anchors of hope so needed as we encounter rough seas on our journey. These anchors were prayed for, sought after, and cherished as she weathered the disruptive circumstances of her life. And now she offers them to others who are weary and need encouragement.

Sandi has written, "God wants us to choose to trust Him with our pain, to focus on Him in the midst of it, and to respond to Him by receiving His offer of healing and hope." Perhaps these were the words she spoke to the dear Polish woman she met who came to a friend's home feeling hopeless, but who left after spending an evening with Sandi by saying, "Now I have hope." It is this hope and trust in God as we enter the rolling waves, this hope and perseverance in the midst of our storm, and this hope and peace in the aftermath of our trial that Sandi desires to impart to all who read this book.

As you read *Anchors of Hope,* you might consider making your home your shelter, having a cup of tea as your beverage, and keeping your Bible near as a constant resource—and oh, perhaps you might need a few tissues, for often tears enable us to reach out and cling to the one and only Anchor who graciously bestows peace and hope as we navigate the storms of life.

*Cynthia Heald*

# SPECIAL THANKS

*To Jan and Evelyn:*

*"Hellooo, are you lost?"* you called out across the road near your home in Surrey, England, on that rare sunlit February afternoon. Moments later we were enjoying tea and crumpets on your settee, sharing our similar storms of life. Your questions led me to tell you about this book I had just begun writing and about my "Anchor of Hope." Little did I know then that He would allow me the joy of returning to England as your overnight guest that we might share further from our hearts. You were there in the beginning. Thank you.

*To Donna, Patty, Alice, Bev, Heidi, Linda, Nancy, Ruth, and others:*
Sisters by birth and/or by "spiritual birthright." Your continual prayers, help, comfort, and support through various storms of life and subsequent stages of growth will always bring a smile to my lips, a song to my heart, a lift to my spirit. God used each of you in special ways to show His love, and I thank you.

*To Carol, Carole, Cynthia, Judy, Kathe, Lael, Lindsey, Mary, Sandra:*
As authors, you have inspired me over the years with your excellent writings. I've laughed and cried and learned and grown from reading your Christ-honoring labors of love. As friends, I will always

treasure the memories . . . how you've pampered me in your homes, encouraged me in my own writing, and allowed me the privilege of being "in labor" with you as your books were being "birthed." Together we've prayed you through final editing and "delivery" deadlines. Then came those glorious moments when the "stork" would drop your bundles of joy on my doorstep, with loving notes on the flyleaf. Thank you.

*To John:*

Your incredible support these past months, as my loving husband, my friend, has allowed me to face the computer screen more than the stove or the time clock. I will always be thankful for your commitment to the Lord and to me . . . and for your belief that I have something to say and the gift of saying it. You are a blessing. Thank you.

*Above all, to the Lord Jesus Christ, my ultimate Friend:*

You know me inside and out, Lord, yet still you love me. Amazing. You sent just the right storms at just the right time . . . then brought Your healing touch, Your strength to persevere, Your grace and mercy. Through it all You allowed me to see You and to know beyond any shadow of doubt that You are my "Anchor of Hope." I praise You, and thank You, with all my heart.

# CONTENTS

# PROLOGUE

## A Valentine Story

Why we were in the Valentine card section at all, only God knows. It was the last place you'd have expected to find us that year. Or for us to find each other.

For me, this would be another Valentine's Day without my "Valentine" at home. Reality hit. And it stung. My eyes began filling with tears.

I looked over at her. Her eyes were filled with tears too. As we talked, I learned that her dad had walked out on her mom two years earlier when the last child in the family had turned nineteen.

I stood there, listening to her sad tale of heartache, rejection, and pain.

"How is your mom coping now?" I asked gently.

Looking at the floor, she answered haltingly, "My mom, well . . . um . . . she died." Apparently after the ordeal, her mom had retreated into a shell—devastated and depressed—then developed a rare form of cancer and died soon afterward. Never able to get a handle on the pain, never finding that anchor of hope, this precious girl's mom was said to have died of a broken heart.

As I walked out of the store, I could not get this young woman and her mother out of my mind. Almost angrily, I cried out to God, "Why couldn't someone have reached this woman in time—*someone!*—to give her Your message of hope? Lord, please, don't let one more person die needlessly of a broken heart. Somehow let them know the Good News that You suffered and died so that we don't have to 'grow weary and lose heart.' "

That was just yesterday.

And today, I am more motivated than ever—compelled, actually—to begin at last, to share the Hope that is in me:

Jesus Christ.

I know firsthand that He is faithful.

## Written in the Clouds

A beautiful hand-crafted plaque graces my desk with these words:

*"Though . . . the hills be shaken, My love shall never leave you."*

—Isaiah 54:10

I took comfort in its message over and over: *"My love shall never leave you."* It was given to me by my husband the first week of October 1990.

The second week . . . he left.

In my aching heart I cried out to God, "Lord, how can this be? He promised his love would never leave me! But it did!" Then God tenderly reminded me about pronouns. "*My* love, precious child, *My* love shall never leave you." And in all these years it has not.

That message is the purpose of this book. It is not to tell of my life but of His life in mine. I even wonder where my life would be today apart from His. Or where my faith would be apart from the storms He has sovereignly, faithfully, allowed into my life.

What are the storms of life? They are difficult times and circumstances that test our faith—custom-designed by God to achieve His greater purpose for our lives.

- They can be physical, emotional, spiritual, relational, mental, judicial, financial. . . .

- They can be the result of someone else's decision or the consequence of our own willful sins or mistakes.

- They can even come when we are doing exactly what God wants us to do.

- They can make us bitter or better, draw us closer to or farther from God, and draw others closer to or farther from God, depending on our response to it.

## *Where Our Storms Connect*

I try to picture you in my mind, dear friend—you who are holding this book in your hands. Perhaps you are experiencing a storm of life, and someone who cares about you has given you this book as a gift. You are blessed to have such a friend.

Or you may have seen the word *Hope* in the title as you wander numbly through the bookstore in need of much hope. I've been there. Although I don't know you or your struggle, I do know the One Who does! He knows. He cares. He will see you through your storm.

"It's amazing, Sandra," I shared one afternoon with Sandra Aldrich, who along with another writer friend, Carol Kent, had been after me for months to put pen to paper. "Everywhere I go, it's as if I'm wearing a sign that says, 'I see you need hope. Can we talk?'"

"There's a title for your book," Sandra replied.

Yes, you're right.

Something about hope.

Maybe hope is something you really need right now.

*Are you just now entering stormy waters?* Maybe it was sudden. You were blind-sided. Maybe you saw it coming. Whatever the case, it can be frightening. Where do you turn? Who can you trust?

*Are you right now in the midst of storm-tossed seas?* Maybe you're doing the best you know how, struggling to keep your head above water while the winds of adversity continue to whirl you about. You need hope! You look within, backward, outward. Where can you find it?

*Are you experiencing the aftermath of a fierce storm of life?* Maybe you're left in the dust, confused, bitter, wondering how to be whole again. You can't imagine any good ever coming from your suffering.

If any of these scenarios describes you—or someone you care about—then read on, dear friend.

This is a book of hope.

King David's prayer for victory in battle can help us prepare for any great storm. Let the Lord Himself be your Anchor as you pray these words from Psalm 20:1-2, 4-5:

*In times of trouble,*

*may the LORD respond to your cry....*

*May He send you help from*

*His sanctuary and strengthen you....*

*May He grant your heart's desire*

*and fulfill all your plans. May we shout*

*for joy when we hear of your victory,*

*flying banners to honor our God.*

*May the LORD answer all your prayers.*

## Where There's Hope

If you are wondering today where to take your broken heart to be fixed, be encouraged: "The LORD's delight is in those . . . who put their hope in His unfailing love" (Psalm 147:11).

Through my own storms of heartache, hopelessness, and helplessness, I have watched with my own eyes as God has provided an Anchor of Hope—strength and direction—then set me on a course of encountering wounded people around the world who needed His hope in their lives too. You'll meet a few of them in these pages. Perhaps you'll see yourself in their stories.

But my storms may be different from yours. Calm compared to most. In his excellent book, *Trusting God Even When Life Hurts*, Jerry Bridges expresses my same thoughts: "Many of my friends have experienced far greater adversity than I have. Who am I to write words of instruction and encouragement to them when I have not experienced the measure of pain they have? My answer to that question is the realization that the truth of God's Word and the encouragement it is intended to give is not dependent upon my experience. It is about God and His sovereignty, wisdom, and love as they bear upon the adversities we all encounter."

Yes, our storms may be different. But our Anchor is the same. Our Hope is in Jesus Christ. So come with me on a journey, dear friend—a journey to healing and hope.

Watch the Lord's divine guidance at work through two real-life drama storms:

- In a small aircraft high in the skies over England.

- In a sailboat on the high seas of Holland.

And experience His amazing love in action in the aftermath of a third storm:

- A storm of life just as real, just as frightening as the first two—the kind most of us are faced with at some point in our lives.

God has many truths He wants to teach us in the course of each storm. Truths about Himself. About us. About our relationship with Him.

*"God is willing to assume full responsibility for the life that is fully yielded to Him."*

—ANDREW MURRAY

# *Part One*

## AT THE ONSET OF MY STORM

*Does God know about my storm?*
Yes, God is all-knowing!

*Does God care about my storm?*
Yes, God is all-loving!

*Can God do anything about my storm?*
Yes, God is all-powerful!

# Trust

*Jesus said, "Let not your heart be troubled;
believe in God, believe also in Me."*
—JOHN 14:1 (NASB)

# "MAYDAY! MAYDAY!"
## Storm in the England Sky

"Zero-two-Lima, Mayday! Mayday! Zero-two-Lima! Do you read me, Tower?

"MAYDAY! MAYDAY!"

The words played over and over in nightmare form long after that fateful day in the sky, when our tiny Cherokee 180 aircraft was unknowingly to encounter gale-force winds over northern England.

We set out, a young couple and our unborn child, on what we thought would be an enjoyable afternoon flight from our home in England up to Scotland to see loved ones. Misinformed of weather conditions, we suddenly found ourselves flying into a severe storm which had grounded all aircraft, including 747s.

Our first clue that we were in trouble (besides the zero-visibility factor) was the fact that we were bouncing around the sky with fierce turbulence from the 70-knot winds. Inside the cockpit we were feeling the impact of every air pocket as our bodies thumped repeatedly against the hard interior, each jolt followed by another thud inside my protruding abdomen. This would not be the time or place I would choose to give birth.

"We're flying over Newcastle," my husband called out to me, "our last chance to emergency divert. Do you want to land or press on?"

"Let's land!" I hollered over the noise of the engine (a reassuring sound, considering the alternative.)

"Let's press on!" he countered. So much for democracy.

But news from the tower soon made the decision for us. The head winds were so strong we would run out of fuel before our next chance to land. So, wisely, we began our descent—totally on instruments and the voice from the control tower as they talked us down.

It was truly Mr. Toad's Ultimate Wild Ride. We never did see the ground, even when we hit. It was unbelievable! A tree had just blown across the runway. Crowds had gathered at the tower to see this young pilot and his wife who had fallen out of the sky during one of the worst storms ever to hit Newcastle. Men ran out to throw sandbags on the plane to keep it from blowing away with the fierce winds.

There are humorous parts of this story, too, which still bring a chuckle (such as the maternity-dress-in-the-wind episode.) Many of life's worst experiences have a way of seeming funny when we view them in our rearview mirror, don't they?

But in those tenuous moments, the most memorable lesson for me was the sightless flying aspect—the intense concentration—relying solely on the dials of the instrument panel and the voice of the tower operator as our only way of knowing where we were and where we needed to be. We couldn't trust our surroundings. They weren't even visible. Instead we trusted our lives to unseen forces: radar and radio waves.

Similarly, as a Christian, I see how much of our lives are based on this same concept: TRUST.

- The instrument panel is like the Word of God. As we read and heed that input from the Lord Himself, we find direction. No matter what our emotions or other people may tell us about our situation, God's Word is the only consistent, reliable source of absolute truth.

- Interacting with the tower is like communicating with God in prayer. As we pray and listen, as we purpose to hear and obey God's voice—His still, quiet voice—we make it through the storm safely.

At the onset of life's storm, we tend to panic and wonder, "Does God know what's happening? Does He even care? Is He able to do anything about it?"

There's only one way to find out: trust, wait, and see.

*You love Him*

*even though you have never seen Him.*

*Though you do not see Him, you trust Him;*

*and even now you are happy with a*

*glorious, inexpressible joy.*

—1 PETER 1:8

# DOES GOD KNOW ABOUT MY STORM?

## HE IS OMNISCIENT, ALL-KNOWING
We need never be afraid to trust an unknown future
to an all-knowing God.

> *O LORD, You have examined my heart*
> *and know everything about me.*
> *You know when I sit down or stand up.*
> *You know my every thought when far away.*
> *You chart the path ahead of me*
> *and tell me where to stop and rest.*
> *Every moment You know where I am.*
> *You know what I am going to say*
> *even before I say it, LORD.*
> *You both precede and follow me.*

—PSALM 139:1-5

## Summer of '74 Adventure

I'll never forget our ten-year high school reunion trip. My friend Shelli and I decided to take all of our preschool-aged children along on the adventure, which meant a three-day drive through several Southern states in an old Volkswagen camper. It was a decision we lived to regret, but we wouldn't trade the memories. Been there?

Never mind the fact that there was no air conditioning, or that the hungry mosquitoes at our first campsite seemed the size of sumo wrestlers, or even that the potty chair dumped out at 70 miles an hour (another story for another time). The memory that remains indelibly in our minds is the night we decided to take the creative route and ended up bumping along a dark back road,

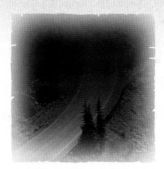

lost, tired, and desperately in need of drinking water and rest rooms.

By this time one of the children had gotten sick. We were unable to see a thing. No stars or moon. Pitch black. Finally we just stopped for the night, seemingly in the middle of nowhere.

But next morning, lo and behold, when our waking eyes had adjusted to the light and we had clambered out of the car to unfold our legs, we saw that we were actually NOT in the middle of nowhere.

We were right in the middle of God's protective care.

Incredibly, we had stopped just short of a cliff. Had our tires rolled a few feet farther the night before, we would have plunged—all six of us—to certain death down a rocky ravine.

We also saw that a few yards in the other direction was a water spigot with fresh water . . . and rest rooms. Civilization.

So I ask you: Did God know about our predicament?

"I guess so, Sandi, but why did He let you suffer all night rather than show you?" some have wondered. It's OK to ask why. God understands. Ultimately, however, some better questions might be: Why did He save us from plummeting down the cliff? Why did He protect us from dehydration, serious illness, accidents, or any number of other potential hazards? Why did He provide so many beautiful sights and sounds along the way? Why did He keep us safe from bears and mountain lions and other varmints that night?

I don't pretend to have answers for why God does what He does or why He allows what He allows. Or why He says *no* when we've cried out for a *yes*. Why some are healed and some are taken home. Why some tragedies that we're certain He could prevent still happen. We are continually surprised by events that take place in this world or in our little corner of it. But the surprises are in what we see, not in who God is. He is the same, yesterday, today, tomorrow.

Nothing in God's creation escapes His knowledge! I am in awe as I read in Psalm 147:3-4: *"He heals the brokenhearted, binding up their wounds. He counts the stars and calls them all by name."*

Wow! There are said to be over a billion galaxies and more than 100 billion stars in our universe. And yet the all-knowing God who counts them and calls them by name is the very One who lovingly bends down to heal our broken hearts! He knows and cares about what is going on in our lives.

Yes, dear one, you may be hurting, asking the *why* questions. People die. They wound us or fail us. They turn their backs on God. Storms of life engulf us. Burdens weigh us down. But God sees, and He weeps with us. He gently reminds us in the midst of our burdens to count the blessings. God knows everything we do, say, think, feel, experience. And He allows us to experience the hard stuff for a reason—a reason we may not understand, but always for a greater purpose.

Who hasn't heard of the patience of Job amid his series of afflictions and wished that we could have it in the midst of ours? Did you catch his extraordinary response to Mrs. Job when she had finally had enough and told her husband to curse God and die?

Wisely, Job replied, *"Shall we indeed accept good from God and not accept adversity?"* (Job 2:10, NASB).

Maybe that's the best question of all.

## Prayer

*Dearest Father*, You tell us in Your Word to trust You with all our hearts rather than depend on our own understanding, and to seek You in all we do—then You will direct our paths (Proverbs 3:5-6). Mostly all we've known is our own self-will and our own way, our own self-sufficiency. Help us desire to seek Your face and trust Your will, Your direction for our lives.

Strengthen each of us to say, as did Your shepherd king David, "I trust in You, O Lord. . . . You are my God. My times are in Your hand" (Psalm 31:14-15, NASB).

Lord God, we're tired and weary. We're numb, fearful. We stumble and fall, trying to make sense of it all. We ache all over, wondering when this storm will pass . . . how we can ever endure this . . . what the outcome will be . . . where to turn for answers. . . .

And so, we thank You that in the midst of all this, You tell us to "Come!"—all of us who are weary and carry heavy burdens—to come to You, and You will give us rest (Matthew 11:28).

*See page 119 for additional Scripture prayers related to this and other chapters.*

# DOES GOD CARE ABOUT MY STORM?

## HE IS COMPASSIONATE, ALL-LOVING

If I were the only lost sheep,

my Shepherd would come to rescue me!

> *"This is what the Sovereign LORD says:*
> *'I Myself will search and find My sheep.*
> *I will be like a shepherd looking*
> *for his scattered flock.*
> *I will find My sheep and rescue them*
> *from all the places to which they were scattered*
> *on that dark and cloudy day....*
> *I will search for My lost ones who strayed away,*
> *and I will bring them safely home again. I will*
> *bind up the injured and strengthen the weak.'"*
>
> EZEKIEL 34:11-12,16

## *A Shepherd's Promise*

A vivid real-life portrait of our Good Shepherd remains forever
in my mind. It was on a back road in northern Italy, during the
season when sheep are led up to high country. My car had stopped
for the flock as it paraded across the road in front of me. What a
treasured sight: newborn lambs in pouches on backs of goats . . .
bleating, baa-ing . . . as they made their way past me, up the hill
to my right.

Seeing the last one disappear over the rising, I started the engine and proceeded down the road. Suddenly from the left, seemingly out of nowhere, a tiny lamb darted in front of my car. I slammed on my brakes, horrified, knowing I could not stop in time—that in a split second my tire would crush her. But then, in that split second, the shepherd appeared. Swiftly he reached out his staff, snatched his lamb from the tire's path, and stood gently enfolding her in the crook of his arm, close to his heart.

I froze, my eyes riveted on the scene before me: the fragile lamb, safe in the strong arms of the burly shepherd. "O Lord," I wept, "how much like that lamb I am, and how much like that shepherd You are. How many times have I unknowingly darted into the path of danger, oblivious to the peril, and You rescued me. Just in time. And You held me close to Your heart. My fierce Protector . . . my loving Guardian . . . my awesome Shepherd."

## Prayer

*You, Sovereign Lord*, are coming in all Your glorious power. You will feed Your flock like a shepherd. You will carry the lambs in Your arms, holding them close to Your heart (Isaiah 40:10-11).

Thank You, dear Lord, that You care for us as a shepherd cares for his lambs, that You gently lead us where You know we need to be—physically, emotionally, mentally, spiritually, financially, relationally. All the while You are teaching, blessing, strengthening, and helping us to know You, to grow in You as we follow You.

One way You do this, we know, is by allowing storms into our lives: sometimes the gentle breezes of ordinary adversity, sometimes frightening gale-force winds. But Your Word tells us that we can rejoice when we run into problems and afflictions because we know they are good for us. They help us learn to endure (Romans 5:3).

How thankful we are that when You—our Good Shepherd—speak to Your own, You never use words of despair, hopelessness, frustration, defeat, discouragement, fear, confusion, or failure. Rather, You give Your sheep words of Hope. Rest. Peace. Victory! Power! Joy! Triumph! And, love.

Thank You, Lord, that there is *nothing* any of us can do to make You love us any more or to love us any less. We are secure in You, our loving Shepherd.

# CAN GOD DO ANYTHING ABOUT MY STORM?

## HE IS OMNIPOTENT, ALL-POWERFUL

God controls both the storms of nature and
the storms of a troubled heart.

### MATTHEW 8:23-27

*Jesus got into the boat and started across the lake
with His disciples. Suddenly, a terrible storm came up,
with waves breaking into the boat. But Jesus was
sleeping. The disciples went to Him and woke Him
up, shouting, "Lord, save us! We're going to drown!"
And Jesus answered, "Why are you afraid? You have
so little faith!" Then He stood up and rebuked the wind
and waves, and suddenly all was calm. The disciples
just sat there in awe. "Who is this?" they asked
themselves. "Even the wind and waves obey Him!"*

## The Restaurant

My heart was crushed, my mind whirling, as I took a seat in the balcony at Glen Eyrie Conference Center in Colorado Springs. That morning was a mixed blessing. I enjoyed being with Shirley Dobson as we sat together, listening to her husband speak to our teens while filming his teaching video series, *Life on the Edge*. But inside I was agonizing over the tough-love message I would be giving that evening to a family member. I believed it was the direct leading of God, but I'd never done any such thing before. Shirley and I talked briefly about it; she encouraged me, and we prayed together.

"What time will you be meeting at the restaurant?" she asked. I told her, and she assured me, "Jim and I will be on our knees praying at 7:30 tonight."

That night I shared my concerns from the depths of my heart as planned, as gently and lovingly as anyone could. But it was not going well. In fact, at the point where all the "frogs" were out of the "bucket"—(all the issues out on the table)—he said he'd had enough and proceeded to leave the restaurant.

But God had other plans.

It had been a calm, sunny day when we entered the restaurant. But by the time he was heading toward the door, a sudden storm had begun raging. The strong winds made it impossible for him to get the door open. "Oh, this is just great!" he sarcastically conceded, crossing his arms defiantly. Standing beside him now, I looked at my watch. It was 7:33. I pictured James and Shirley Dobson on their knees, praying to our creative, sovereign God on our behalf.

The longer we waited, and the harder he tried to push the door open, the greater the winds blew. It literally became humanly impossible to open that door. He pushed again with all his might. No way. Then came the hail. Finally, he decided we might as well sit back down and wait out the storm.

So we returned to our table, where everything was still in place— the tip, the tea bags . . . and all the issues of the heart. We began talking and putting the "frogs *back* into the bucket" one by one. When we finished with the last one, and shut the lid, the storm

subsided as suddenly as it had begun. The rain stopped, the wind grew calm, the sun came out. And we walked out, reconciled.

Some might say it was just an interesting coincidence.

For me it was the powerful hand of our awesome, sovereign, gracious God, who controls both the storms of nature and the storms of a troubled heart in response to the loving intercessory prayers of His people.

Dear friend, are you in a situation that looks impossible? Do you feel like you've prayed to God time and again with no seeming results? Does your storm of life seem so fierce you assume that God has lost control, that you're at the mercy of the "winds of fate"?

Be encouraged: God is in His heaven. He is sovereign. He is all-powerful. Not only does He have control over the entire universe and over all of history but over your own personal day-to-day circumstances as well. Just as Jesus calmed the waves, He can calm whatever storms of life you may be facing.

Put yourself in the sandals of Christ's disciples for a moment: you're an experienced sailor, you know the real dangers of a storm like this, and you're scared! How could Jesus be sleeping at a time like this? You've seen Him work miracles before in other's lives. Why won't He try doing anything about this enormous problem in yours?

He wants to help us if we'll only ask Him. We may not be spared the pain or suffering. But God will see us through, no matter how terrible our storm. Ultimately, His purposes for our lives will be fulfilled, and we will be at peace. His plans for us are good and full of hope!

This promise of restoration extends to you, my friend, and to all God's people wherever they may be found.

*"My eye is not on the density of the fog,*

*but on the living God who controls every*

*circumstance of my life."*

—GEORGE MUELLER

## Prayer

*Almighty God,* this is what You've said to us: All this may seem impossible to us now—to us, a small and discouraged remnant of Your people. But do we think this is impossible for You, the Lord Almighty? No, no—we can be sure that You are going to rescue Your people. You will be faithful and just toward us. So we will take heart and finish the task (Zechariah 8:6-9).

Father, thank You for Your all-knowing, all-caring, all-powerful nature! None of this ever escapes You. You are not wringing Your hands wondering what to do. You have everything under Your sovereign control. You meet us where we are, You see our pain, You comfort our hearts. You love us with an everlasting love. You show us where to look as we seek Your face.

# Part Two

## IN THE MIDST OF MY STORM

*Where am I focusing?*
Seeking His face.

*What am I learning?*
Gaining His wisdom.

*Who am I impacting?*
Shining His light.

# Focus

*Let us run with perseverance the race
marked out for us. Let us fix our eyes on Jesus,
the author and perfecter of our faith.*

—Hebrews 12:1-2 (NIV)

# "LAND IN SECHT!"
## *Storm on the North Sea*

"Hurry, we're going to miss it!" our Dutch friend Maarten shouted, as we ran—(like fools)—headlong into a storm on the North Sea. This was sure to be the experience of a lifetime, he assured us. And this "captain" of our four-man sailboat was not about to let any of us miss out on it.

We had docked for a refreshment break and had begun to see people—the *smart* people—run for cover as the dark clouds gathered and the winds picked up. But like fish swimming upstream, we headed out to sea while all the others were hurrying ashore to safety.

If I'd ever wondered what a bottle cork on wash-cycle must feel like, I needed wonder no more. Tossed about by the waves, we ventured farther and farther out to sea until we could no longer see land. I was terrified.

If I looked at the blackened sky, I was scared.

If I looked at the angry waves, I was frantic.

If I looked at the impossible circumstances, I was mortified.

Suddenly, I looked at Maarten. He had a grin from ear to ear. He shouted, "Wow! Isn't this GREAT? This is fantastic!!"

Hmmmm. Let's see here. The circumstances around us are about as frightening as they can possibly get. And the one at the controls is having a *really good time*.

What am I missing here?

Without even realizing what I had done, I had switched my focus from the sky, the waves, the water-filled boat. Instead, I had fixed my gaze on Maarten, the one with the rudder controls in the palm of his hand, the one with a gleam in the center of his eye. And I found peace . . . because the one who was in control was at peace.

When I took my eyes off Maarten and focused on the brewing storm or the angry waves, I would panic. But when I focused on him and his gleeful countenance, I had peace. So my eyes became riveted on Maarten's grin.

Suddenly, lightning flashed. Then the thunder roared its rapid response! Maarten's grin turned downward. I was in trouble.

*Where in the world could I look NOW?*

We were no longer having fun. Not even Maarten.

The next terrifying moments involved all of us straddling the boat as the waves mercilessly, repeatedly, threw our craft skyward. Being on the very end, I was thrown higher than the other three, so just before the wave would engulf us each time, I could see farther than anyone. It was then that Maarten taught me my first Dutch phrase: "Land in secht!" I was to scream it as soon as I saw land.

Since I am the one recounting this event, you've already guessed that we survived. But I learned something very important on that afternoon adventure, something that would later see me through other storms in my life:

*Focus!*

Friend, I wonder where you feel *your* gaze is fixed right now, in the midst of your present storm . . .

- Is your focus backward—at the shores of your past?
- Is your focus inward—at the relentless hurt?
- Is your focus outward—at the hopeless circumstances?
- Or is it upward—at the One who can give you Hope, even in the midst of your storm?

> *"We are not promised smooth sailing,*
> *but a safe landing."*

—ADRIAN ROGERS

# AM I LOOKING BACKWARD?

## WE CAN'T CHANGE THE PAST

Forgiveness allows a person to come to terms with his past
in order to embrace his future.

COLOSSIANS 3:13 (NIV)

*Bear with each other*

*and forgive whatever grievances*

*you may have against one another.*

*Forgive as the Lord forgave you.*

## The Reunion

At our 35th high school reunion, true confessions were rampant:

- "I had a secret crush on you. . . ."
- "Remember that rumor . . . ?"
- "I was the one who got you in trouble. . . ."

The first night of the reunion, a distinguished looking "older man"—(ahem)—spotted me and made his way through the crowd. "Sandi! Finally! After 35 years! I have to apologize to you. We have to talk!"

*Oh dear. Who is this? And what could he possibly have harbored all these years?*

As he approached, I peeked at his name tag: "Walter E. von Stouffel." *Wally?* I'd heard he was now a prominent surgeon on the East Coast. But to me, he was simply Wally. Prom date, circa 1963.

I motioned over to the nearby swimming pool. Twenty class-mates began trailing us. A true confession was about to be made, and they weren't about to miss out!

"Sandi, you'll never know how many times I've kicked myself for not walking you to the door that night," he began. "I'm so sorry! I left you standing by the car. . . . My mother never taught me. . . . I feel so bad. . . . Can you ever forgive me?"

*Wow. Go easy on yourself, Wally.* I could picture him in the middle of surgery over the years: "Sponge. Scalpel. OH NO, I CAN'T BELIEVE I DIDN'T WALK SANDI TO THE DOOR!"

I felt suddenly responsible. "I forgive you, Wally. I forgive your Mom. Let's clear the slate and get on with life!" He beamed, sighed with relief, and floated back into the crowd. A burden lifted.

*Forgiveness.* I thought that night about the fresh beauty of it, about the newness of life that can result from it. If Wally's countenance could take on a new look after being released from such triviality, I wondered how many of us could leave our reunion weekend behind with not only a new look but a new life? How many of my childhood friends needed God's life-changing forgiveness that night?

We don't know who will be around for the 40th reunion.

*"God can free us from any burdens in our past that still hold us captive, whether sin we committed or sin that was done to us."*

[CYNTHIA HEALD]

We've already lost far too many of our 512 classmates over the years. Vietnam, car accidents, illnesses. But this particular night we had the opportunity—the privilege—of "clearing the slate." Of encouraging and inspiring each other in special ways. Above all, of sharing the good news of God's love and forgiveness—a free gift, available just for the asking. The Apostle Paul grabbed the opportunity in Acts 13:38-39:

*"Brothers, listen! In this man Jesus there is forgiveness for your sins. Everyone who believes in Him is freed from all guilt and declared right with God."*

Freed from all guilt. All of it.

• *Do you need some of that forgiveness?*

Psalm 51 is David's cry to God following his sin of adultery. He knew the importance of putting his heart right with God once again. Yes, sin—ours and the sins of others toward us—can leave many innocent people in its cruel wake. Ultimately it is an offense against God, a rebellion against His way of living. When, like David, we are the offender, we must do as he did—turn to our merciful God, confess, and be cleansed in order to receive His forgiveness and be restored to fellowship with Him. He may even direct us to set things right with those we've wronged.

• *But what if we are the one who's been wronged, or someone we care about*—the innocent victim left in the wake of others' hateful, hurtful acts? Everything in us can try to hold on to that pain, reliving the hurts, nursing our wounds, or taking up an offense on behalf of the mistreated one. Most of us have experienced this at some time in our lives. We want to punish those who hurt us. We want to make them pay. Yet in doing so we end up punishing ourselves by remaining a victim. And we pay the price.

Forgiveness, like healing, can be a challenging process. But if we allow God to work in and through us to develop a forgiving spirit, we can begin to heal from the inside out. Marie Eades writes,

*"When I truly forgave and could pray for those who had hurt me, I experienced a healing power from that prayer that I cannot put into words."*

Focusing on a past we cannot change can lead to bitterness, resentment, and anxiety. It keeps us in bondage. But God wants to release us from that bondage, to free us to be whole again, experiencing His peace, embracing His joy, moving forward in His strength, one step at a time. Praying for God's hand to guide us through this difficult but crucial process will ultimately benefit not only us, but also those who love us.

Dear friend, are you suffering, as Wally was, with pangs of

guilt over a mistake or wrongdoing in your past? Remember what 1 John 1:9 tells us, "If we confess our sins to Him, He is faithful and just to forgive us and to cleanse us from every wrong."

Or are you the victim of someone's unjust treatment of you? Are you struggling with one or both sides of the forgiveness coin? Tell the Lord how you're feeling, let Him show you what to do, and then take comfort in His Word.

*"Sometimes the Lord calms the storm.*

*But sometimes He lets the storm rage,*

*and calms the child."*

[BILLY GRAHAM]

## Prayer

Father, I know that if I confess my sins to You—my faithful One—You will completely forgive me and thoroughly cleanse me (1 John 1:9). So I bring my sins before You, Lord. I rid my hands of them. And I ask that You would bring to my attention any wrongdoing that I have perhaps unknowingly committed against You and against others.

But Lord, You know very well that others have also sinned against me. And You know what a hard time I've had releasing my feelings of hurt and loss and anger. But by Your Holy Spirit's power in me, I choose today to forgive those who have sinned against me, for if I do not forgive them, I cannot truly walk in Your forgiveness (Matthew 6:14). Let me never give in to the temptation to repay anyone evil for evil but to live at peace with them, if at all possible on my part. Help me not to avenge myself but to leave room for You to do Your perfect work (Romans 12:17-19).

Father, with Your help I am focusing all my energies on this one thing: forgetting the past and looking forward to what lies ahead (Philippians 3:13).

For all the right reasons. For Your honor and glory.

## WE CAN'T ALWAYS CONTROL OUR CIRCUMSTANCES

Joy is not the absence of suffering but the presence of God.

### JAMES 1:2-4

*Dear brothers and sisters, whenever trouble comes your way, let it be an opportunity for joy. For when your faith is tested, your endurance has a chance to grow. So let it grow, for when your endurance is fully developed, you will be strong in character and ready for anything.*

## Grounded in Joy

During a particularly painful time of life for me, I happened to be traveling through Denver. To my surprise, my daughter met me at the airport gate during my layover, bearing a gift bag, a smile, and a hug. Inside the bag was a beautiful card and a collection of thoughtful items that expressed her love for me . . . including a matching journal and bookmark with colorful, cascading flowers and the following words:

*"Abiding joy does not depend upon what is happening around us. It exists because of the One who is living in us."*—B.J. Hoff

What an encouragement and a timely reminder! We who have the power of the living God residing inside of us need not succumb to worry over our desperate circumstances. He will give us joy. Abiding joy! Not only after the victory but in the midst of the battle.

We've all been there . . . in the depths of despair . . . afraid, angry, depressed . . . looking hopelessly at what we call our "impossible" circumstances.

Maybe you're there now.

As you look around, you've already determined that the waves are too huge. Your boat is too small. The clouds are too black. There's no land in sight. Gloomy darkness enshrouds you, as you sink deeper. And deeper. And deeper.

If only there were a way out of these circumstances. If only! If only! But if we were to look into the face of the Captain of our ship . . . and listen carefully . . . we could hear Him whisper to our heart, through His Word, in the midst of our storm, "Be still, and know that I am God" (Psalm 46:10, KJV).

When I recall those terrifying moments in the middle of the North Sea, I remember the literal highs and lows we experienced when we were thrown high into the air one moment, only to plunge rapidly downward to the depths, engulfed in the angry waves of the sea.

Then I think about daily life, with its ups and downs, its rolling waves of circumstance. When things are going well, we are on a high. Life is good! But when adversity hits, we may sink into depression or despair. The great news is that joy, which comes from a consistent life in Jesus Christ, rises above the highs and lows. When our lives are in His, we can survive even the highs of prosperity, as well as the lows of adversity, and remain level and calm as though the waters around us were smooth.

It's not denial, my friend. It's joy. It's not putting on a happy-camper mask, or gutting it out in our own strength, or covering over the pain, or any number of other defense mechanisms we manage to dream up in order to persuade ourselves and others that we're happy. It's joy—abiding joy in Christ—no matter what is happening around us. We know His love is constant. He not only cares about what we're going through, He can do something about it. We can therefore rest in His love . . . and experience abiding joy in Him.

## Prayer

Father, like the Apostle Paul, I feel like I am being pressured in every way. I feel perplexed, persecuted, struck down by this horrible storm. It feels like I'm dying inside. Lord, I need to know that I am not going to be crushed, or left in despair, or abandoned, or destroyed. I admit that I feel very weak today, like a clay jar, but perhaps this is as You want it—so that there will be no doubt that it is *Your* extraordinary power sustaining me in my storm, rather than anything coming from me (2 Corinthians 4:7-10).

Help me understand that You have not only given me the experience of believing in You but also of suffering for You (Philippians 1:29). And whatever I must suffer, I want to walk through it with my eyes focused on You, who will never fail me or forsake me.

## WHEN WE CAN'T BEAR THE PAIN

God's unconditional love is the salve for all our wounds.

### PSALM 147:3

*He heals the brokenhearted,*

*binding up their wounds.*

## The List

I used to have a list. It was a long list, not on paper but rather in my mind. Invisible to the eye but lethal to the heart. I would rehearse this list upon rising each morning and at various times throughout the day. It was a list of ways this person had hurt me and caused me grief. It did not bring me joy or relief from pain. On the contrary, it only made me more bitter, more miserable with each recitation.

Then one day God came alongside me with His own list.

"Yes, Sandi," He whispered in my heart, "this person is unloving. But I am Love." And then He gave me a verse.

"Yes, this person is rejecting you, but I am rejoicing in you." Then He gave me another verse.

And so it went.

"Yes . . . untruthful, but I am Truth . . . unfair, but I am just . . . brings hurt, but I bring healing."

For every negative, God supplied a positive . . . and a verse to go with it. I suddenly realized He had done a marvelous thing: He had taken away my old list, and I never saw it again.

I had a new focus. A list of God's attributes is what I began to wake up to each morning, praising Him for Who He is, thankful that He cared enough for me to replace my spirit of bitterness with His spirit of forgiveness. I began to be whole once again. Forgiveness had taken root. This doesn't mean that I never get down or discouraged or try to resurrect those hurt feelings now and then. Sometimes I do. But when those moments come, God speaks to my heart: "Oh, don't you remember, beloved? I AM LOVE." And again the verse flows from my lips. Often through tears . . . of joy and thankfulness.

His list has become a balm for my heartache.

*Heartache* is a common term, immortalized in classic literature and country/western songs. But only when you have been intensely wounded emotionally do you realize the true meaning of the word. There is a literal ache in your heart, an indescribable crushing pain inside that seems to strike at the deepest level, at the most unwelcome time.

Where do we go with this uninvited pain? Too often we internalize it; we send it underground. Outwardly, we pretend it isn't there or that it doesn't matter. Or we try to hold on to our hurts until they begin to define who we are, eventually overtaking every waking moment of our lives. We are rendered useless, helpless, defeated.

But our God is not a God of defeat. He is a God of victory. And He wants us to live victorious lives. As we allow His pure, unconditional love to penetrate our aching hearts, we find its presence to be a soothing salve.

Dear friend, are you feeling that knife in your heart so sharp you don't think you can endure it? Can you identify with Barbara Johnson's words in the midst of her gut-wrenching pain?

*"All the promises of God are there, and they're real, and they're true, but right now you're bleeding, you're raw and hurting, and you have to hang on to those promises even if they don't seem to work for you at the moment."*

Jesus understands. He was no stranger to heartache. The Bible says, "He was despised and rejected—a man of sorrows, acquainted with bitterest grief. We turned our backs on Him and looked the other way when He went by. He was despised, and we did not care" (Isaiah 53:3).

We can choose to focus inward at our hurts or choose to allow His love to be the salve, to soothe and bring healing.

*"Heartache forces us to embrace God out of desperate, urgent need. God is never closer than when your heart is aching."*

[JONI EARECKSON TADA]

"*We can hug our hurts*

*and make a shrine out of our sorrows*

*or we can offer them to God*

*as a sacrifice of praise.*

*The choice is ours.*"

[RICHARD EXLEY]

## Prayer

*Lord God,* sometimes it seems I can't bear the crush of my spirit, the ache of my heart. When King David wept with grief, Father, You strengthened him by Your Word (Psalm 119:28).

And so I turn to You and Your Word with my hurting heart. How I thank You, dear God, that You are right here with me, that You delight in having Your little girl crawl up into Your lap and nestle into Your strong arms, as You comfort me with Your words of promise:

You keep track of all my sorrows, Lord. You have collected all my tears in Your bottle (Psalm 56:8). Lovingly You remind me that You rescue those who are brokenhearted and crushed in spirit (Psalm 147:3), and that Your gracious favor is all I need, because when I am weak You are strong (2 Corinthians 12:9). Only You know what I long for, Lord, as You hear my every sigh (Psalm 38:9). You love me with an everlasting love, and draw me close to You (Jeremiah 31:3).

And so I praise You—even in the midst of this painful time. For You are my source of power, courage, and wisdom. Nothing can separate me from Your love (Romans 8:38).

## CHANGING OUR FOCUS

The Lord wants us to have peace in the storms of our life
as we are hurled to and fro by winds of adversity.
He wants to give us courage, grace, strength, joy, and victory.

JOHN 14:27 (NIV)

*"Peace I leave with you; My peace I give to you.*

*I do not give to you as the world gives.*

*Do not let your hearts be troubled*

*and do not be afraid."*

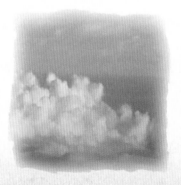

## The Grand View

One of the best parts about flying a lot is getting continual glimpses of God's perspective.

We drive to the airport through torrential rains, we fight the stormy blasts of wind while awaiting the shuttle bus to the terminal, we board the plane and take off through dense fog. All we know from our limited view is that life is gray, dismal, cloudy, dark.

Then, that glorious moment, when the plane breaks through the clouds and levels off. Radiant sunshine! Above the clouds, everything is sunlit, cheery, clear, and bright.

Our perspective is so different from God's! What we see as grim, He sees as glorious. We see but a tiny part of the picture of life. He has the Grand View!

From high in the sky, I can't help but sigh as I gaze down at the hustle-bustle of life, the backed-up rush-hour freeway traffic from whence I've just come. It's a fresh look at my own earthly problems and gives new meaning to the saying that no predicament is too big for God's intervention, no person too small for His attention.

Before my friend Mary died of cancer, she taught us all some amazing lessons of faith and the value of looking up in the midst of suffering. She taught us about her "Thankful Game." It began the day she left the doctor's office with the news of her terminal illness. She cried out to God as she drove down the road toward the mountains.

"Oh, Mary," the Lord began speaking to her heart, "I know your sorrow. I love you. I will be with you. I have many things I want to teach you through this. The first is a lesson on thankfulness."

"Thankfulness, for what, Lord? This cancer? Never!" she cried.

"Then what can you be thankful for? Name one thing, Mary."

She looked up. It was a gorgeous spring day. "OK. Thank You for the blue sky, Lord," she sniffled. Then she added, "And for the beautiful sunshine." She looked out at the fields in bloom. "And thank You for those colorful flowers. And the mountains." Before long, Mary was on a roll, thanking God for many things in her life. The moment came when, yes, she even thanked Him for the cancer. Whenever she got down, or afraid, or overwhelmed, she remembered to look up, thanking God for the sky . . . and the rest would begin to flow from her lips.

Thankful indeed, Mary was, for the cancer that enabled her to impact the suffering, lost, and hopeless of the world for Christ—*hundreds* of them before she went Home to be with Him.

Why is it important to keep looking up . . . in the midst of our storms? Because when we do, we are promised His peace. Isaiah 26:3 tells us that God will keep in perfect peace all who trust in Him, whose thoughts are fixed on Him.

When the disciples got caught in a sudden storm on the Sea of Galilee, they were terrified. Then Peter saw Jesus walking toward them on the water, calling him to come. Peter stepped out on the water, his eyes riveted on Jesus. But as soon as the storm grew strong, Peter's faith grew weak. "He was terrified and began to sink. 'Save me, Lord!' he shouted" (Matthew 14:30).

He changed his focus back to the Lord, and he was saved.

"When one minute we're clearly focused," Charles Stanley writes, "and the next minute we're floundering around in search of something firm to anchor us, what helps us regain our bearings?" King David knew the answer full well! When he would panic in the midst of a storm, yield to temptation, and be lured away from the Lord, toward sin, he was quick to refocus his life by seeking God's forgiveness and guidance. No matter what he had done, he was never too prideful to return to the Lord.

Dear friend, are you needing peace in the midst of your storm? Jesus tells us to have peace in Him. "Here on earth you will have many trials and sorrows. But take heart, because I have overcome the world" (John 16:33). Peace comes when we're walking in step with the God of all Peace . . . focused on Him, trusting Him to see us through our storm. This means fixing our eyes, not on our problems, but on the Lord—praying expectantly for wisdom and direction from the only One who sees the big picture!

*"Do you know Jesus? If so, run! Fix your eyes on Him and refuse to give up or turn back. If not, stop! Give Him your struggles and receive Him by faith."*

[CHARLES SWINDOLL]

## Prayer

O Lord, help me to remember to look up, to see You, to acknowledge Your many blessings and promises, and to thank You even for my storm . . . and for Your peace in the midst of it.

Heavenly Father, when I seek Your face, focusing on Your beauty, Your power, Your majesty, then my troubles seem to diminish, and Your light begins to overcome my dark world. Just like Peter, my faith and focus may have been upward at one time, but somewhere along the way, I lost it, Father God. Help me, please, to refocus upward, toward You.

And now, open my eyes, dear Lord, that I may see clearly all that You have for me to see. Open my ears to hear Your quiet, reassuring voice. Open my mind and heart to all those things You long to teach me . . . in the midst of my suffering.

## GAINING HIS WISDOM

What we call "God's waiting room" is really His classroom!

JOHN 16:12-13

*"Oh, there is so much more I want to tell you,*

*but you can't bear it now. When the Spirit of truth*

*comes, He will guide you into all truth."*

## God's Waiting Room

One day I was writing in my personal journal that I had begun many months earlier with the title *Reflections from God's Waiting Room*. As I reviewed page after page of what I'd written, I realized this had been more of a learning time than anything. So I scratched out the phrase *Waiting Room* and replaced it with a new word:

*Classroom.*

Yes, there were countless lessons being taught through my months of waiting:

- I was not allowed time to sit and thumb mindlessly through magazines. God had me on my knees and in His Word.

- He showed me the importance of actively seeking His face, His wisdom, and His counsel while He was blessing my life with friendships along the way—His children who were supporting, encouraging, and praying for me.

- He had me learning such principles as trust, focus, obedience. He began a process of molding and shaping me in order to create a heart for Him, a heart that He wanted to become more contrite, thankful, tender, forgiving, and understanding. Whenever I'd failed or faltered or fallen flat, He had me busily learning about humility, perseverance, and the patience to wait for His timing.

On one page I had written these words, as David had in the Psalms, "How long, O Lord, how long?" And then I had added, "It's been four years, Lord!"

I chuckled as I read those words five years later, while still in His waiting room—oops, I mean, classroom.

James 1:2-4 says, *"Whenever trouble comes your way, let it be an opportunity for joy. For when your faith is tested, your endurance has a chance to grow. So let it grow, for when your endurance is fully developed, you will be strong in character and ready for anything."* Notice that James doesn't say *if* trouble comes your way but *when* it does. We will have storms, but we can benefit from them. We are encouraged here to turn our hardships into times of learning. Tough times can teach us patience and build character in us.

Please understand that the last thing I want to try to offer is a series of pious platitudes. We get enough of those from well-meaning friends and loved ones, whose reminders that "God will work all things together for good"—while true—leave us cold at the moment of crisis and pain.

God is big enough to take care of all the things we can't. He calls us to lean on Him, to give it all to Jesus. But at the same time, He wants us to be actively involved. Not to toss Him the ball and say, "OK, you've got it now," then go lie on the couch and pull the covers over our heads until the crisis passes. Rather, we can be honest with Him about how we feel, allow Him to comfort us, and then await further instructions.

Healing can begin as the Lord directs and empowers us to join Him in the process. And Pain 101—the class no one signs up for but everyone benefits from—is usually the source of the greatest education of our lifetimes. We learn who God is, who we are, and who He and we can be together.

God is interested in our discovering His fullness, and that's what can happen in the midst of trials.

~

*"Our initial reaction to trials and adversity is a good indication of where our trust rests. If we run to others or begin panicking when difficult days strike, we need to stop and immediately ask, 'What does God want me to learn from this difficult situation?'"*

[CHARLES STANLEY]

## Prayer

*O Lord,* tell me again, please—we can do this, You and I, can't we? I confess that at times I get so impatient with Your process of molding and shaping me that I feel like trying to jump off Your potter's wheel or climb out of Your fiery furnace—to go where the lessons come less painfully. Yet I know that the safest place to be is in the center of Your will and that You have me here for a reason, a greater purpose.

So I pray for endurance in the midst of this storm. Help me not to become weary and give up—but to look up instead—to wait upon You, Father, knowing that I will gain Your wisdom and reap Your harvest at the proper time (Galatians 6:9).

You promise, Lord, that as I wait on You I will find new strength. I will fly high on wings like eagles. I will run and not grow weary. Teach me to wait, Lord, patiently expecting that You will fulfill Your promises in Your perfect way, in Your perfect timing. Strengthen me to rise above the storms of life as I trust completely in You (Isaiah 40:31).

# WHO AM I IMPACTING?

## SHINING HIS LIGHT

We may be the only "Bible" some people will ever read.

### PHILIPPIANS 4:9

*Keep putting into practice all you learned from me*

*and heard from me and saw me doing, and*

*the God of peace will be with you.*

## The Happy Bible Ladies of 204

The doctor faced me squarely with shocking words:

"Possible brain tumor."

And thus began the subsequent flurry of preparations for exploratory surgery and checking into my hospital room.

I looked over at the empty bed beside me. *Who would be assigned as my roommate? What was her physical problem? Moreover, what was her spiritual need?* Whatever it was, I was ready and eager to give an account of the hope that was in me, with gentleness and respect (1 Peter 3:15).

I had arrived armed and dangerous with assorted gift Bibles, devotionals, Good News booklets, Billy Graham's *Peace with God* tracts in various cover styles. You name it, I had packed it, fully confident that God would answer my prayers for just the right roommate.

Finally, here she came. As we began getting acquainted, you can imagine my shock—and hers—when we discovered we were both Christians, and both had come prepared to share the gospel with the roommate we had prayed for.

Surely there was some mistake.

We went together to the nurse's station to remedy the obvious mix-up. "No mistake, ladies. You are both assigned to 204." We shrugged, grinned at each other, and settled into our room to enjoy some great moments of fellowship as newfound sisters in Christ. In the ensuing hours we laughed and cried together as we shared from the depths of our hearts.

*Sara and Sandi, reporting for duty, Sir.*

But this story is not about us. It's about our faithful God. What was to transpire in the following days was an extraordinary picture of God's goodness, wisdom, and sovereignty. He knew what we did not know: that we would need each other's support and encouragement as we faced the unknown, that we would need each other's fervent prayers as we were each wheeled into surgery. And beyond our own needs, others were also there with needs to present to God's throne of grace.

We knelt together by my bed in our hospital gowns in prayer for the nurses and doctors. We'd hear them come in, then tiptoe out. We'd keep praying.

I remember standing in the gap for other patients in that ward we had met who were facing crises and needed a touch from the Lord, even just a listening ear or friendly smile. "Girl, you're a Welcome Wagon hostess in a gown and slippers," Sara chided me that next afternoon. "Look who's talking?" I chuckled. "How many miles you got on that wheelchair?"

We were labeled the Happy Bible Ladies of 204, presumably

because we had our Bibles open most of the time and laughed a lot. Those who knew what we were going through had to understand the connection between the two. Or maybe they thought we were in denial, since our situations did not warrant a lot of humor, humanly speaking.

Our joy was supernatural. It came from the same faithful God who was orchestrating something bigger than us or our problems, something wonderful in the midst of our pain, something totally outside of our own doing. We knew beyond a doubt that this was where we were supposed to be. This was all part of His plan. And we were along for the ride of a lifetime.

The moment came for Sara to go home, and she turned over her remaining "ministry assignment" to me before she left. "Amber in 208 . . . long, dark hair . . . she's 16, not married, pregnant, physical complications, emotional too . . . abandoned by her boyfriend, rejected by her family, no friends . . . she's all alone . . . she's scared." My heart ached for this girl I was yet to meet. Sara and I hugged and said our good-byes.

"Lord, show me. Make the way clear to . . ." I looked up from my prayer to see Amber passing my door, carrying her coat and bag, headed for the lobby.

*Oh no, she can't go yet!* Throwing on my robe and slippers, I grabbed a Bible and bag of tracts and scuffed hurriedly down the hallway, down the elevator, and found her seated by the front door of the lobby, staring out the window.

Funny—when you're on a mission, you don't think about what people think or what you look like. You just go.

Sitting down beside her, I looked into her frightened eyes. And it seemed the Lord just took it from there, opening up her heart and mind to what I longed to share with her.

I prayed that the taxi would delay until we were finished.

"You feel all alone, and hopeless, and scared. God understands. He loves you and knows what you're going through. And y'know what? He can help you through this hard time." I held out the Bible to her. "He tells you in here that you don't ever have to feel afraid. It's His Book of promises, to encourage you, to give you direction when you don't know where to turn. You and I don't have any answers, but He does. If you trust Him and give Him your heart, He promises that you will never be alone!"

Tears of compassion welled up in my eyes as I looked into hers and began to quote from Isaiah 41:10: "Do not fear, for I am with you; do not anxiously look about you, for I am your God. I will strengthen you, surely I will help you, surely I will uphold you with My righteous right hand" (NASB).

Her face brightened, her eyes softened, alluding to what God was surely doing in her heart. She would go somewhere to think over what she had heard, talk to God, and read her new Bible, starting with some marked verses.

It was a divinely orchestrated moment.

I like to think that somewhere today there is a 38-year-old Christian mom, kneeling in prayer with her godly son or daughter, praising God for that life-changing day in 1981 when He came into her shattered life, mended her broken heart, and together—hand-in-hand—began their journey of hope.

I picture her praying now: "Lord, just as You promised You would that day, You helped me . . . strengthened me . . . upheld me. You took my loneliness and fears, replaced them with new mercies, new life. Your Word comforted me, restored me, carried me through valley times, then showed me where to turn. My child and I want to thank You, to devote our lives to serving You, to tell all who will listen, about God our loving Father who gives us hope, in the midst of every 'hopeless' situation."

~

I know what you're thinking: *I can barely keep my head above water, and now you're suggesting that I should throw a lifeline to someone else who's drowning?*

Not exactly. But be aware that God can use you while you're in the midst of your storm to impact others in ways that you'd be unable to do at any other time.

Second Timothy 2:20-21 says, "In a wealthy home some utensils are made of gold and silver, and some are made of wood and clay. The expensive utensils are used for special occasions, and the cheap ones are for everyday use. If you keep yourself pure, you will be a utensil God can use for His purpose. Your life will be clean, and you will be ready for the Master to use you for every good work."

While we are busy learning and growing through our trials, we can be sure others are busy watching . . . observing our lives, for good or not-so-good . . . our attitudes, our actions and reactions. If we keep ourselves pure, we will be utensils God can use for His purpose. Our lives will be ready and available for the Master to use us for anything.

Even in the midst of . . . everything.

# CATCH YOUR BREATH

As we come to our third and final section, let's review the important concepts from the first two real-life-drama storms:

1) *Terror in the Skies*

TRUSTING one's life to unseen forces of radar and radio waves demonstrates the need to trust our lives to the invisible, invincible Almighty God.

• The instrument panel . . . like the Word of God.
• The communication with the tower . . . like prayer.

Talk to God! Grow to know Him as you saturate your mind and heart with His Word.

2) *Tempest on the Seas*

FOCUSING on the One who holds the rudder of our lives in the palm of His hand brings peace to our hearts.

In the midst of our storms, it's crucial where we fix our gaze:

- Not back at the past
- Not outward at the circumstances
- Not inward at the hurt

Look up! Ask God to teach you what you need to learn through this, then shine your light!

And now, the rest of the story—where we all live . . .

## 3) *Tethered in the Harbor of Hope*

RESPONDING to God's offer of help brings hope to our lives. Following both of the real-life drama storms we've talked about, there was closure. The winds died down, the plane flew back. The sun came out, the boat was docked. But what about the aftermath of a storm of brokenness—a broken heart, a broken dream, a broken home, a broken body, a broken relationship? The storms have died down, but the wreckage is all around.

How do you respond to the storms of death, divorce, disaster, depression, disease, disability, dread, doubt, deceit, disloyalty, distrust, destitution, depravity, desertion, disappointment, destruction, despair—these devastating storms of life—when they come upon you or someone you care about?

There are no easy answers. But in the aftermath of any storm of life, we have a place of refuge—a safe harbor—as we allow the Lord to be our Anchor of Hope, and as we remain tethered to Him!

Remember King David—mighty warrior, giant slayer, powerful ruler. Was it the conflicts on the battlefront that burdened him so? No, it was the battles on the home front that brought him to his knees, time and again. Read the psalms of David. They are filled with his anguish, stained by his tears, as he agonized over trials of his heart and home:

- The death of his infant son, his best friend Jonathan, his grown sons

- Betrayal, rebellion, corruption, immorality, heartache within his family

- Guilt from his own sinful actions against Uriah, Bathsheba, and others

- Fleeing for his life from his friend-turned-enemy Saul, and even from his own son

- Suffering the pain of slander, hatred, rejection, betrayal, of friends and loved ones

- Failures as a father, a husband, a man—storms that could cause anyone to sink!

Think about this: If David was so deplorable in his weaknesses and sins, why does God lovingly call him "a man after God's own heart"? And if God allowed David to grieve and suffer such losses as loved ones, health, reputation, and relationships, why does David declare, "I will praise the Lord at all times"?

David had a secret. It is revealed in over 70 of his psalms: a hunger and thirst for God and His Word.

David's response to the tragic events of his life and their lingering aftermath was to turn them over to his sovereign God.

To TRUST God. To cry out and repent.

To FOCUS on God. To rely on Him, praise Him, beseech Him, love Him, seek His forgiveness, meditate on His Word, and ask Him the hard questions.

Then to RESPOND. To thank God for His answers, for His strength, His comfort, His powerful works, His presence, His faithfulness, His forgiveness, the beauty of His creation, the wonders of His love, and—mostly—His HOPE!

Amid the storms of his life—the tragedies and defeats—David responded by turning to God in his pain. And God responded by drawing close to David and teaching him some profound lessons about Almighty God Himself, which David recounts for us in the Psalms:

- "From the LORD comes deliverance" (Psalm 3:8, NIV).

- "God is my shield, saving those whose hearts are true and right" (Psalm 7:10).

- "God is my helper. The Lord is the one who keeps me alive!" (Psalm 54:4).

- "I will sing about Your power. I will shout with joy each morning because of Your unfailing love. For You have been my refuge, a place of safety in the day of distress" (Psalm 59:16).

- "When I am afraid, I put my trust in You. . . . I praise Your word. I trust in God, so why should I be afraid? What can mere mortals do to me?" (Psalm 56:3-4).

- "You are my place of refuge. You are all I really want in life" (Psalm 142:5).

- "O God, You are my God; I earnestly search for You. My soul thirsts for You; my whole body longs for You in this parched and weary land where there is no water" (Psalm 63:1).

- "The sacrifice You want is a broken spirit. A broken and repentant heart, O God, You will not despise" (Psalm 51:17).

- "Have mercy on me, O God, have mercy! I look to You for protection. I will hide beneath the shadow of Your wings until this violent storm is past" (Psalm 57:1).

- "To the faithful You show Yourself faithful" (Psalm 18:25).

Dear friend, are you struggling like David with the aftermath of storms on the home front? Do you suffer from guilt over storms you brought upon yourself or others, or from grief over storms of loss? Are you experiencing painful relationships? Fearful unknowns?

Take heart—and read on! You'll discover that God has a plan for you . . . peace for you . . . hope for you.

~

*"Come to Me, all of you who are weary and*

*carry heavy burdens, and I will give you rest.*

*Take My yoke upon you. Let Me teach you,*

*because I am humble and gentle, and*

*you will find rest for your souls."*

MATTHEW 11:28-29

# Part Three

## IN THE AFTERMATH OF MY STORM

*Will I see Your hand in my storm?*
Acknowledging His plan.

*Will I praise You for my storm?*
Experiencing His peace.

*Will I tell of You after my storm?*
Sharing His hope.

*Hope*

*"For I know the plans I have for you," says the* LORD.
*"They are plans for good and not for disaster,*
*to give you a future and a hope.*
—JEREMIAH 29:11

# "CAST ANCHOR!"

*Tethered in the Harbor of Hope*

When my daddy left our home, just before my eighth birthday, I didn't realize that I would never see him again. Twenty years later, I stood by his flag-draped coffin, listening to his Naval war-hero accomplishments . . . and grieving the daddy I never really got to know, the one who never really got to know his little girl.

Friends and family who had known my father always told me how I resembled him.

"Oh, you're just like your daddy," Grandma had lovingly said, cradling me in her arms.

"Oooh! You're JUST like YOUR FATHER!" Mom had scolded me one day out of fatigue and frustration.

But I didn't know him.

So I had two recurring questions—two longings—that burned within my childish heart:

*1) Who am I?* Am I good, like Grandma declared, or bad, like Mommy implied? I longed to know my daddy . . . so I could know who I was.

*2) Will I ever get to sit in his lap and be his little girl again?* I longed for Daddy's hugs, feeling safe and secure in his strong arms.

Maybe you can relate to some of these personal childhood memories. Maybe you have your own version, your own story involving your earthly father. Perhaps there are scars from abuse, abandonment, or addiction—or a distance between the two of you, geographical or emotional. Maybe you've been separated because of death or divorce, duty or imprisonment. Chances are, your earthly father did the best he knew how, but due to his own struggles, from childhood or later years, he was unable to be the Daddy you longed for.

No matter what our stories, our questions, our longings, we are not without HOPE, because our heavenly Father has stepped in and given us a priceless gift: Himself.

Shortly after Daddy's funeral, I found Christ. I became a daughter of the King! And now I had answers to my two persistent questions:

1) I discovered thousands of word pictures in Scripture of who God is. I know now who I am because I know *Whose* I am.

2) My longings are fulfilled, infinitely more than I could have imagined, as I crawl into the lap of my Heavenly Father, nestle into His loving arms, and delight in His hugs.

In the aftermath of devastating storms of loss on my own home front—as daughter, mother, and wife—I have found the Lord to be my all-sufficient Anchor. I have experienced firsthand God's plan, His peace, His hope . . . and this truth:

*Neither the loss of my daddy when I was 7,*
*nor the loss of my baby when I was 27,*
*nor the loss of my husband when I was 47,*
*could cause wounds too deep for my Abba Father to heal.*

"Abba" Father—"Daddy" Father. A beautiful picture from the Bible. Unlike our earthly father is able to be, He is always perfect. Always loving. Always available. Always wise and fair. We can trust Him to keep every promise. He will never leave us or forsake us. His character is holy and pure. His Spirit is one of love, joy, peace, patience, kindness, goodness, faithfulness, gentleness, and self-control. No matter how godly a dad may be, he can never measure up to this perfection! Only our Heavenly Father can.

Our plan for our lives never includes parents who desert us, children who die, marriage partners who break their vows to us, or countless other trials of life. But we live in a fallen world, and when we are faced with these storms and their lingering aftermath, we must make choices. God wants us to choose to trust Him with our pain, to focus on Him in the midst of it, and to respond to Him by receiving His offer of healing and hope!

So why not crawl up into your Daddy-Father's lap right now and talk to Him? If you love Him and long to know Him better, tell Him! Thank Him for who He is and what He's done for you. Share with Him what you're thinking, where you're faltering, how you're feeling. Tell Him your dreams and longings, your fears and failures, and whatever else is on your heart. He already knows, of course. But He wants you to be open and honest before Him. He will draw you close to Him, comfort you, and become your most cherished Friend.

As a child of the King, you need to know how special you are—precious and honored in His sight. Your Heavenly Father longs to spend time with you, to listen to your hurting heart, and begin its healing process.

The One who knows you best loves you most!

# WILL I SEE YOUR
# HAND IN MY STORM?

## ACKNOWLEDGING HIS PLAN

God brings people and circumstances into our lives
to prepare us for a future that only He can see.

### JEREMIAH 29:13

*"If you look for Me in earnest,*

*you will find Me when you seek Me."*

## The Transformation

I stepped from the car at the Washington, D.C., airport, having just received one of the most crushing blows a woman could ever be dealt. Numbly, I made my way onto the plane, eyes red and swollen, openly sobbing, as if I had just lost my best friend. Indeed, in my mind I had.

I'll never know who on that plane saw the transformation. Someday I'd like to meet with the man on the aisle who hastened to let this "out-of-control-woman-in-crisis" into the window seat, with a look of panic in his eyes. He could give an eyewitness account of the miracle God performed that day, inches away from him in the course of that three-hour flight, with just a Bible, a pen, and a journal.

We all have an imaginary portrait on the canvas of our mind, a picture of who we are. Over the years I had allowed society, self, circumstances, peers, loved ones, and others to paint on my canvas . . . to show me who I was. More recently that picture had been painted over to become a portrait created flawlessly over time by a loving Master Artist, stroke upon stroke, color upon radiant color. Each brush stroke had revealed a truth—a biblical description— of who He was, and thus who I was in Him.

But on this particular afternoon, at that airport, it was as if one cruel and deliberate yank of the easel had sent the portrait crashing to the ground. It lay shattered in a thousand pieces. Settled into my airplane seat by the window, still sobbing, I began to pray . . . then slowly opened my Bible . . . then numbly reached for my journal and pen. . . .

Pages turned, ink wrote, tears dried, more pages turned, countenance changed. I prayed, and read, and wrote, and prayed, and wrote . . . and read more intensely . . . more joyously. . . . Gradually, a smile replaced the dismal frown. By the time the plane landed, the easel of my mind had been uprighted, the picture recreated. New truths were added from the Word of God that day to create a portrait more resplendent than ever before. God had miraculously transformed me from the inside out. And I walked off that plane with a smile on my face and a testimony on my lips, to the glory of God.

God had been there.

And God was still there.

My hurt hadn't gone away. It was real. It was tangible. But I had seen the Truth of my situation in the pages of God's Word and in the Hope of my ever-present Father. I didn't know exactly where I was going, but I knew God was going there with me.

And that was all I really needed to know.

## Prayer

Thank You, dear Heavenly Father, for the portraits in Your Word that show us who You are, and thereby who we are in You. Thank You that you care so deeply for us, even when we blow it, or when we fail to love You as we should. Thank You for your discipline, for loving us enough to correct us . . . and forgive us. Thank You that even in our most unlovable moments, when we stumble and fall, You reach down, pick us up, dust us off, wrap Your strong arms around us, and embrace us as Your beloved children. Thank You for the testings, the trials, that cause us to draw closer to You. And in the midst of them, thank You for providing for us a haven—a harbor—of hope!

In Your precious Son's name, Amen.

~

*"When we're experiencing storms of life, we ask, 'How does God fit into the picture?' God does more than just fit into the picture of our lives. He creates it, reshaping it into something that will bring glory and honor to His name."*

[CHARLES STANLEY]

# WILL I PRAISE YOU
# FOR MY STORM?

## EXPERIENCING HIS PEACE

If we have experienced great pain,

we have the potential to offer great praise.

PSALM 30:1

*I will praise You, LORD,*

*for You have rescued me.*

## Wonder in Warsaw

It was 6:15 a.m., and I was headed home. My weeks of ministry in Eastern Europe had been wonderful, but now I was ready to be back in America. Stepping out of the taxi at the Warsaw airport that morning in late November, I was met with a face full of snow as it blew sideways with great force. What was to follow was NOT in my itinerary. But it was in God's.

For some unknown reason, the ticket I had in my hand would not work. And the train ticket I had as a backup to get me to Vienna, where I could fly on a non-Polish plane, was nowhere in my possession. In the course of the morning, surrounded by rushing people with foreign accents, by constant loudspeaker announcements in various languages, I had dumped out all my bags looking for the ticket and had gone from one end of the airport to the other, from airline to airline, trying to solve my problem.

Nothing.

Finally, an agent at Air Italia wrote a name and address on a piece of scratch paper: *Luigi. Such-and-Such Travel Agency.*

"Signora, perhaps he can, uh, how you say . . . help your troubles?"

*OK, Luigi, you're on.*

In desperation I snatched the directions and proceeded on a course that would involve three bus transfers, a brisk walk up and down streets and back alleys in Old Town Warsaw, carrying luggage through sideways snow, looking for street signs that would lead me to the tiny travel agency and the agent who would be able to rescue me.

At last I arrived and began pouring out my story to Luigi and his colleague. In the course of an hour, they managed to tell me "no" in three different languages. They would not take a credit card to buy a new ticket. They would not accept phone cards to call someone in the States who could rescue me. All man-made solutions to my problem were ripped out from under me. I looked in final desperation at the two agents. They were shrugging their shoulders, shaking their heads. Gripped with the reality that I'm going to be spending the rest of my life in Warsaw, the tears began to flow.

The only Polish phrase I could think of at the moment was, "Gdje yest toaletta?" (*"Where is the ladies' room?"*) They pointed to a door which led down to a dungeon. As I began my descent down the stairs, I started to pray, "Oh Lord, I thank you that you are here with me. I thank you that you can understand every word I speak. Thank You for Your love . . . Your care . . . Your faithfulness in my life. Thank You . . . praise You . . . thank You Lord for . . . praise You, Lord. . . ." And on it went.

When I came back up and walked through the door, I was truly a new creature. The tears had dried and there was a joyful countenance on my face, which seemed perplexing to the two agents.

*Hmmm. She left in tears, she came up smiling.* They looked at each other, then one of them disappeared through the door to find out what was down there that made me so happy. Perhaps he's still looking. Because there was nothing down there to make anyone smile. The joy had come from INSIDE of me. My circumstances were no better—WORSE, in fact, if anything—because by now all the flights out of Warsaw had left. So perched on a chair by the window, I watched the falling snow, listened for the Lord's still, quiet voice, and continued silently praising.

Nearly an hour had passed when a phone number suddenly came to my mind! It was the number of the young Polish Christian woman who had kindly let me sleep on a mattress in her apartment somewhere in Warsaw the night before. I explained the situation over the phone to her and asked, "If I could find a taxi who could ever find your apartment, could I stay tonight?" She replied, "Yes, of course you can stay with—*Oh dear!* I am so sorry, but I have some women coming to my place tonight for a Bible study and . . . Oh! . . . *OH! You come and give testimony?*" I said that I would be glad to share whatever the Lord would lead, to which she added, "Don't worry, I'll translate. I know your Polish, it's no good." She was right! The taxi delivered, the group arrived, and it was truly a God-ordained evening.

Two women remained after the Bible study. The Lord opened the floodgates and DEEP sharing began to flow from my lips. I didn't know of their woundedness. I later found that my story was very similar to theirs. I didn't even know their names, but I could see their pain through their tears as I shared about the Lord, about what He had done for me and what He would do for them.

At the end of the evening, the first woman, Eva, came up and said through tears, "Oh Sandi, I come tonight with no hope. You give me hope!" I told her, of course, that it was the Lord who had given her hope. "I'd have been on a plane over the Atlantic right now. But God loves us all so much, He wanted us to have this time together. He is a good God, Eva."

"Oh yes—*good* God, *good* God!"

The other woman, Marysha, took my hand and said, "I come tonight and I think nobody love me, nothing to live for. Now I know! Jesus, He love me! I live for Him, yes?"

"Oh yes, Marysha!"

We had a group hug, group prayer. I did not understand a word of it, but I didn't need to. The One to Whom they were speaking understood every word.

The next morning, the ticket miraculously worked, everything fell into place, and I flew home. Surely I could've flown home without the plane, I was on such a spiritual high.

Our God is to be praised at all times. And He in turn can bring peace, joy, adventure, growth, usefulness, delight, beauty, purpose, new friendships, and countless blessings into our lives. And into the lives of others.

~

*"Adversity is a part of life. It can be a friend or a foe, depending on how we approach it."*

[DAVID JEREMIAH]

## Prayer

*Dearest Father,* praise comes easily with each fresh reminder of Your goodness, Your protective care, Your bountiful provision. Let me never become so complacent, so prideful as to think that I am the center of my life. You alone are the Lord most high. You alone are worthy of our praise (1 Chronicles 16:25).

In the Book of Daniel, You inspire us with the words of those three courageous men before they were thrown into the fiery furnace. "The God whom we serve is able to save us. . . . But even if He doesn't . . ." (Daniel 3:17-18). Wow! Even if You don't rescue us in the way we would choose, Lord, may we go on serving You, praising You as we face our own fires of affliction. May we trust You—as they did—knowing that Your way is always best.

As I continue praising You, may I one day reach the place where I can honestly say to You: "Father, I don't want You to remove this storm from my life until You have used it to accomplish all You desire—in me and in others." Looking back, I see time and again where You have done just that. It was Your way, Your timing. And I praise You!

# WILL I TELL OF YOU
# AFTER MY STORM?

## SHARING HIS HOPE

What God teaches us in the dark,
He intends for us to share in the light.

### PSALM 107:29-32

*"LORD, help!" they cried in their trouble,*

*and He saved them from their distress. He calmed*

*the storm to a whisper and stilled the waves. What a*

*blessing was that stillness as He brought them safely*

*into harbor! Let them praise the LORD for His great*

*love and for all His wonderful deeds to them. Let*

*them exalt Him publicly before the congregation*

*and before the leaders of the nation.*

## I Know How You Feel

I have a dear friend who prays for me every time I travel. She prays for all the usual things, of course—for my safety and a smooth, successful trip. But more importantly, she always prays for whoever will be sitting next to me. She fervently prays for God to orchestrate something special. And because He delights in showing Himself faithful, He has answered many of these ordinary prayers in extraordinary ways.

I recall one in particular. A young nurse was sitting by the window on a flight from New York to Denver. She had poured out her life story to me . . . before we had even left the tarmac! It was like my story, seven years earlier. As I listened and relived those emotions with her, it was as if the scab had been ripped from my heart and it was bleeding, aching all over again.

Suddenly I realized what was happening to my face. I had tears streaming down my cheeks—AND a large GRIN from ear to ear. I reached over, touched her arm, and said gently, "I am so sorry. You're getting a mixed message here. My heart aches with you because I remember that pain of rejection. My eyes are filled with tears for you because I know how you are hurting. But my mouth and my mind have already moved ahead . . . to the HOPE I know you can have in the midst of your hurt . . . the Hope I found in Jesus Christ. Would you mind if I shared that with you?"

In the course of the next three hours, this precious young woman listened as I told her all about the Lord. His faithfulness. His strength in my weakness. His love, His wisdom, His sovereignty. His grace and His mercy. How even when it seems we're all alone and no one understands, or cares, or is able to help us, He can. And He will.

By the time the plane landed, she wanted that same Lord in her life.

Do you see the beauty that comes wrapped in the thorns in our lives? Had God not brought me through those very same difficulties, those very same feelings, what would I have had to offer her? Oh, I could have said, "Wow, sounds like you're going through a hard time. What is your name? I'll pray for you."

And I would have. But how marvelous to see the power of the Apostle Paul's words from 2 Corinthians 1:3-6 at work:

*All praise to the God and Father of our Lord Jesus Christ. He is the source of every mercy and the God who comforts us. He comforts us in all our troubles so that we can comfort others. When others are troubled, we will be able to give them the same comfort God has given us. You can be sure that the more we suffer for Christ, the more God will shower us with His comfort through Christ. So when we are weighed down with troubles, it is for your benefit and salvation! For when God comforts us, it is so that we, in turn, can be an encouragement to you.*

The Apostle Paul is an inspiration to us all. He suffered through literal storms, persecution, and many other trials, including a personal weakness—a "thorn in the flesh." And through it all he told of God's faithfulness. Paul's response to suffering helps us to see God's character, that His strength is sufficient for any storm.

God's comfort: what does it involve? Does it mean He makes our problems go away? Usually not. If it did, wouldn't we tend to turn to Him just for pain relief rather than out of love and devotion? God's comfort more often involves giving us His strength, help, encouragement, presence, and hope to get us through our tough times. The tougher they are, the greater His comfort.

Are you feeling overwhelmed, in need of His loving touch? Then tell Him. Let Him give you the comfort He longs to give you. As you experience His comfort in your time of need, you will be able to comfort others in theirs.

## Prayer

*O Father,* how sweetly You comfort us in our storms, then lovingly call us to offer that same comfort to another in the midst of hers (2 Corinthians 1:3). We rarely know just when or how it will happen. But we can count on You—in Your perfect timing—to put a hurting soul in our midst and then summon us to be that "someone with skin on" to love her with Your love.

It may be a person we know. Or a total stranger. When we least expect it, we may be called to comfort a battle-weary child of God with a tender gesture—a smile, a touch, a hug—a kind deed, a word of encouragement.

May we be ready, Lord. Open our hearts to her need. Open our ears to her unspoken cries. Open our minds to recall those times when You came alongside us in the form of a caring friend or stranger, to deliver Your message of hope to us.

And then, Lord, open her heart to *receive* all that You long to give her—through those of us You allow the awesome privilege of being Your vessels of hope in a hurting world.

# CONCLUSION

*Dear Friend,*

You and I have journeyed together through these pages. We have discovered truths about God, about us, and about God and us together, through the inevitable storms of life. I conclude our journey with a summary of these principles, as found in the words God had spoken to me through a stream one day, words about:

- Trust—seeking God and discovering His all-knowing, all-loving, all-powerful character

- Focus—looking up, learning much, and making an impact on others

- Response—encountering obstacles in our path, yet finding hope, seeing God, praising His name, and telling others about Him

It happened several years ago when I was on a mountain retreat. What a glorious spring morning it was—the birds chirping, the flowers blooming. I had found a secluded spot by a stream where for 360 degrees all around, there was no man-made thing in sight. I had just settled down for my time with the Lord when suddenly, out of nowhere, a tiny hummingbird appeared in front of me . . . my favorite little creature! He hovered momentarily, looking at me as if to smile and say, "Hello! God sent me to tell you He loves you. Enjoy your time with Him!" And he flitted off.

Well, I did enjoy my morning with the Lord. As I meditated on His Word and watched the stream, He began showing me, one after another, parallels between the stream and our Christian life. . . .

# The Stream

And God asked the mighty stream to show me how the fullness
of the Christian life is likened unto it, and the stream said:

"Watch me. And learn from me, precious child:

"Flowing full, and confident, along a path yet unknown to me.
Still, I move onward:
Continually yielding . . . trusting . . . going somewhere.

Not looking back, with regret,
Nor forward, with fear and hesitancy,

Because the Master, in all His creativity and wisdom,
Has chosen this path just for me.

"Do you trust Him that much, beloved?
Do you remember to thank Him for your path?

"I leave no thing unaffected in some way, no matter how small.

"Some things, I merely make moist.
In others, I cause growth.

"Still others are permanently affected by me over the course of time:
Obstacles that once were rough, I gradually make smooth.

"Beloved . . .

    Do you have a lasting effect on those whose lives touch yours?

"And speaking of obstacles—

    Those rough, jagged, unexpected rocks,

        Which cause a painful detour in my steady flow—

    Those are what really make me the work of art

        That beckoned you to come to me this day.

"Without them, you would see no waterfall,

    You would not hear my music,

        Nor feel the refreshing splash upon your brow.

"Your delight in me is found . . . not in my smooth places,

    But in my response to the rough spots God has placed in my path.

"Oh, beloved . . .

    Are you thanking Him for the obstacles in your life?

"Look! Over there! Just beyond the boulder—

    That stagnant pool of water!

        It lies still, with no path it need follow,

    No obstacles to cause it to stumble,

        No demands on its time, or forces of energy.

"Yet, there it lies:

    Green. Lifeless. Useless. Ugly.

        And with a stench.

"You quickly look away from it,

    And focus once again on my crystal-clear, flowing waters!

"In me, you see fullness of life . . . continuous blessing,

    Usefulness, beauty, delight to your soul!

"Oh, watch me. And learn from me, precious child:

    Trust the Master.

        Move confidently in Him.

    Affect your surroundings.

        Be useful for His glory.

"And finally: rejoice in the rough spots.

    For, as God has used mine to draw you to me this day,

        He wants to use yours to draw others to Himself.

    He gave me to you today.

        He loves you so."

## A Final Prayer

Heavenly Father, the storms of life surround me, but I will not be tossed to and fro. For I am anchored in Your steadfast love.

*As the storm clouds gather . . .*
I will TRUST YOU, Lord. I will not feel afraid, as I nestle into the protecting arms of my all-knowing, all-loving, all-powerful God.

*In the midst of the storm . . .*
When the raging waves of emotions and circumstances overwhelm me and I feel there is no hope in sight, I will look up and call on Your name, Lord—You, who promise Your peace in the midst of my storm. Help me, please, to keep my FOCUS on You . . . to LEARN what You want to teach me through this, and to let Your LIGHT—your beacon of hope—shine through me to a watching world.

*And then, Lord, as the storm subsides . . .*
Help me to SEE Your sovereign, loving hand in it, and let my song of PRAISE to You echo throughout the ages, from generation to generation, TELLING of Your faithful love, Your awesome deeds . . . that I might have the privilege and joy of sharing the hope I found in You with others in need.

Thank You, dear Lord, for longing to be my Anchor, my Hope, through every storm of my life.

In Your Son's victorious name, Amen!

# SCRIPTURE PRAYERS

## 1. At the Onset of My Storm

*Dear God,* as David did, I cry out to You as I face this crisis, this storm of _____. I'm trusting You, Father, You who know all about this and care what happens to me, to work it out according to Your perfect will, in Your perfect timing. Do not stay silent. Don't abandon me now (Psalm 35:22). You are great, Lord, and You enjoy helping Your servants (Psalm 35:27).

*Lord,* I weep with grief; encourage me by Your word (Psalm 119:28).

*Dearest Father,* I know this storm has the potential to overwhelm me, but I am overcome with joy because of Your unfailing love, for You have seen my trouble, and You care about the anguish of my soul. You, Lord, have set me in a safe place (Psalm 31:7-8). My future is in Your strong and righteous hands.

*Thank You, Lord,* that to all who mourn, You will give beauty for ashes, joy instead of mourning, praise instead of despair. You have planted us in Yourself to be strong and graceful oaks for Your glory (Isaiah 61:3).

*Lord God,* thank You for the encouragement of Your word, which tells us that when we pray, You listen and answer our prayers. You show us Your unfailing love in wonderful ways, saving those of us who seek refuge in You. You guard us as the apple of Your eye. You hide us in the shadow of Your wings (Psalm 17:6-8).

*Lord,* You have promised that You will not leave us comfortless but that You will come to us. Thank You for Your Holy Spirit, our Comforter and Counselor, who abides with us forever (John 14:16-18).

*Thank You, Father,* that when You command us to be strong and of good courage, to be neither afraid or dismayed, You follow it with this promise: "For the LORD your God is with you wherever you go" (Joshua 1:9).

*Lord,* You tell us to trust in You with all our heart and not to lean on our own understanding. Help me in all my ways to acknowledge You, and I know that You, Lord, will direct my paths (Proverbs 3:5-6).

*Yes, Lord,* we are to trust in You, our rock (2 Samuel 22:3). For Your way is perfect, all Your promises prove true, and You are a shield for all who look to You for protection (2 Samuel 22:31).

*Father,* I need to trust You to calm my fears, especially toward certain people in my life. Your Word says that it is better to trust in You than to put confidence in people (Psalm 118:8). You assure us that when we do trust in You, we need not be afraid of what man can do to us (Psalm 56:11), because You will shield us with Your wings, shelter us with Your feathers, and Your faithful promises will be our armor and protection (Psalm 91:4). O thank You, Lord!

*Tell me again, Lord . . .* we can do this, You and I . . . can't we? Your gracious favor is all I need. Your power works best in our weakness (2 Corinthians 12:9). Thank You for this great promise!

## 2. In the Midst of My Storm

*Dearest Father,* in the midst of this storm of _____
I come to You, desiring to seek Your face, to know Your truth, to gain
Your wisdom, and to be a shining example to others, for Your glory.

*Thank You, Father,* for Your Word which is a lamp for my feet and a
light for my path (Psalm 119:105). In its pages we find beauty, truth,
direction, strength, comfort, encouragement. . . .

*You tell us, Lord,* that we are the light of the world, like a city on a
mountain, glowing in the night for all to see. As Your followers, we are
under constant scrutiny, especially by people who do not share our faith.
And sometimes we get weak and weary. Help us, though, not to hide our
light under a basket, but instead to put it on a stand and let it shine for
all. In the same way, may our good deeds shine out for all to see, so that
everyone will praise You (Matthew 5:14-16).

*Strengthen us for the task, Lord,* for we know it is both a responsibility
and a privilege to represent Christ to those who need Your comfort and
salvation (Philippians 1:29).

*Lord,* we pray, as David did, "Teach me Your ways, O LORD, that I may
live according to Your truth! Grant me purity of heart, that I may
honor You" (Psalm 86:11).

*Ah, Sovereign Lord,* You have made the heavens and the earth with
Your great power and outstretched arm. Nothing is too hard for You!
(Jeremiah 32:17).

*Lord,* we want to be strong in Your mighty power—to put on all of Your armor, so that we will be able to stand firm against all strategies and tricks of the devil. May we use every piece of Your armor to resist the enemy, so that after the battle we will still be standing firm (Ephesians 6:10-18).

*Thank You, Lord,* that we can rejoice when we run into problems and trials, because we know that they are good for us. They help us learn to endure, which develops strength of character in us, and character strengthens our hope (Romans 5:3-4).

*God,* You know our frame; You know that we are but dust (Psalm 103:14). Forgiveness is hard, yet You give it to us, and You enable us to extend it to others. Help us to seek it—and receive it. The more we know You, the more we understand Your forgiveness (Ephesians 4:32).

*Father God,* Your Word tells us that "in quietness and confidence" is our strength (Isaiah 30:15). We pray for opportunities to retreat to a quiet place of rest and peace, as Jesus did on earth, especially just before and after major decisions. Speak to us, Lord, as we draw away, so we can see and hear much more clearly about how to go ahead.

*Father,* according to Your Word, if we need wisdom—if we want to know what YOU want us to do—we are to ask You, in faith, and You will gladly tell us (James 1:5). And so we come asking, Lord, with a heart that desires wisdom from You.

*How we praise You, Lord,* that You who began the good work within us will continue Your work until it is finally finished on that day when Christ Jesus comes back again (Philippians 1:6).

## 3. In the Aftermath of My Storm

*Dear Lord,* as we recover from the pain and anguish of our storm, help us, we pray, to see that Your hand has been with us in our storm. Help us to acknowledge that You have a plan for us, and it is good. Help us to remember to sing praises and tell others about You—as You have brought us safely through the storm stronger, wiser, and with renewed perspective—as we have gotten to know You better and have seen a glimpse of Your glory.

*Almighty God,* I know You can calm the raging storms of life, bringing them under Your control with Your powerful yet hushed voice, when I read in Your Word about Jesus calming the storm, "the great storm of wind . . . the waves beat into the ship, so that it was now full. And He was . . . asleep on a pillow: and they awake Him, and say unto Him, Master, carest Thou not that we perish? And He arose and rebuked the wind, and said unto the sea, 'Peace, be still,' And the wind ceased, and there was a great calm" (Mark 4:37-39, KJV).

*Even now, Lord,* I hear You whisper to me, "Be still, and know that I am God" (Psalm 46:10, KJV).

*Please help us, Lord,* not to worry about anything, but instead to pray about everything . . . to tell You what we need, and remember to thank You for all You've done. If we do this, You tell us that we will experience Your peace which is far more wonderful than our human mind can understand. Thank You that Your peace will guard our hearts and minds as we live in Christ Jesus (Philippians 4:6-7).

*Lord God,* Your servant, the shepherd king David, called upon You time and again, knowing You would come to his aid. We pray now as he did: "I will rejoice in You, LORD. I will be glad, because You rescued me. I will praise You from the bottom of my heart. LORD, who can compare with You? Who else rescues the weak and helpless?" (Psalm 35:9-10).

*Father God,* along with David, I declare that unless You had helped me, I would soon have died. I cried out, "I'm slipping!" and Your unfailing love supported me. When doubts filled my mind, Your comfort gave me renewed hope and cheer (Psalm 94:17-19).

*Lord,* as David prayed, "I will thank You, LORD, with all my heart; I will tell of all the marvelous things You have done. I will be filled with joy because of You. I will sing praises to Your name, O Most High" (Psalm 9:1-2). O Lord, have mercy on me. See how I suffer. Save me so I can praise You publicly, so I can rejoice that You have rescued me (Psalm 9:14).

*O Lord,* how I love the promise in Your Word that tells us that You know the plans You have for us. They are plans for good and not for disaster, to give us a future and a hope (Jeremiah 29:11). You go on to say that when we pray, You will listen. If we look for You in earnest, we will find You when we seek You. (Jeremiah 29:12-13). You are truly an awesome God!

*Father,* help us to look at our problems in the light of Your power instead of looking at You in the shadow of our problems. You have set apart the godly for Yourself. You will answer when we call to You (Psalm 4:3).

Praise You, Lord!

*Net proceeds from this book
will be donated by the author
to projects that minister to women in need.*